M.R. JAMES'S

A Warning to the Curious

Peter Leigh

Published in association with The Basic Skills Agency

Hodder & Stoughton

A MEMBER OF THE HODDER HEADLINE GROUP

Acknowledgements
Cover: Dave Smith
Illustrations: Jim Eldridge
Photograph of M.R. James © The Mary Evans Picture Library

Orders: please contact Bookpoint Ltd, 39 Milton Park, Abingdon, Oxon OX14 4TD. Telephone: (44) 01235 400414, Fax: (44) 01235 400454. Lines are open from 9.00–6.00, Monday to Saturday, with a 24 hour message answering service. Email address: orders@bookpoint.co.uk

British Library Cataloguing in Publication Data
A catalogue record for this title is available from The British Library

ISBN 0 340 74312 3

First published 1999
Impression number 10 9 8 7 6 5 4 3 2 1
Year   2005 2004 2003 2002 2001 2000 1999

Typeset by Fakenham Photosetting Ltd, Fakenham, Norfolk.
Printed in Great Britain for Hodder & Stoughton Educational, a division of Hodder Headline Plc, 338 Euston Road, London NW1 3BH by Redwood Books, Trowbridge, Wiltshire.

About the author

M.R. James was born in 1862
and died in 1936.
Many people think he is the best writer
of ghost stories there is.

About the story

At the time this story was written,
people were very interested in the past.
They liked to dig things up,
and hunt for treasure.
This story is a warning
not to dig too far!

Seaburgh is the place
I want you to think about.
It's on the east coast.

It is not very different now
to how it was when I was a child.
It's very flat,
and there are marshes, heath,
a long sea front, a street,
and behind that a large flint church.

flint is a type of
stone

If you walk away from the church,
past the station,
you come to slightly higher ground,
and a ridge that runs towards the sea.

At the end of the ridge by the sea
is a clearly shaped mound.
It's crowned by a little knot of trees.

And here you may sit on a hot spring day,
and look out at the blue sea,
the green grass, the cottages,
the church, and a distant martello tower.

martello towers
were round towers
built on the coast as
look-outs

I used to go to Seaburgh a lot
to play golf,
but I don't go there now,
after what happened on my last visit.

It was in April when I was there,
and the hotel was almost empty.
After dinner one evening
I was in the sitting room
when a young man put his head
round the door.

'May I come in?' he asked.

'Of course,' I said.

'Oh thank you,' he said,
and sounded relieved.

relieved – pleased
and thankful

He came in and sat down.
It was clear he wanted company.
He was nervous and restless,
so I asked him what was the matter.

'You'll think it very odd of me,'
he said, (this was the way he began),
'but the fact is,
I've had a bit of a shock.'

I said he should have a drink,
to calm himself down,
and ordered us one each.

He jumped when the waiter came in,
but then settled back with his drink.

He said his name was Paxton,
and he wanted some advice.
'Of course,' I said.
'What's the problem?'

'It began,' he said,
'more than a week ago.
I'm interested in old buildings,
and was looking around the church.
I was looking closely at a coat of arms
when the rector came in.

The rector asked me if I knew
the meaning of the coat of arms.
It had three crowns on it.
"Yes," I said, and explained I thought
it was the arms of the old kingdom
of the Anglo-Saxons.

rector – a priest

Anglo-Saxons – the first English people

4

"That's right," he said.
"The people here believe
the crowns are holy.
They say they are buried
in different places along the coast,
and they protect us against invaders,
Danes or French or Germans.
One of the crowns was dug up long ago,
another has been covered by the sea,
but the third is buried here in Seaburgh,
and is still doing its work,
keeping off enemies."

"Do they know where it is buried?" I asked.

"They do," said the rector,
"but they won't tell.
But they do say that the crown
guardian – protector   has some sort of guardian."

"A guardian?"

"Yes!"

That was what the rector told me,
and you can imagine how
interesting I found it.
When I left him,
the only thing I could think of
was how to find the crown.

I wish I'd left it alone.

Well, it didn't take me long
to find out that the crown
must be in the mound by the sea.

I know something about digging
in these mounds.
I've opened many of them before.

But that was with the owner's leave,
and in broad daylight
and with men to help.

Here I had to survey the mound
very carefully before I put a spade in.

Still the soil was very light
and sandy and easy.
The main problem would be
the going out and coming back
to the hotel at odd hours.
When I had decided
on the best way to dig up the mound
I told the people at the hotel
that I was called away for the night,
and spent it out on the mound.

I made a tunnel into it.

I won't bore you with how
it was done, and filled in again,
but the main thing is
I got the crown.'

I cried out with surprise.
No one had ever seen
an Anglo-Saxon crown.
'You have the crown?'

'Yes,' he said, and looked
at me unhappily,
'and the worst of it is
I don't know how to put it back.'

'Put it back?
Why, my dear Paxton, you have made
one of the most exciting finds
ever heard of in this country.
Of course it must go
to the British Museum.
What's the problem?
If you're thinking about
the owner of the land,

treasure-trove –
the laws about
buried treasure

and treasure-trove and all that,
I can certainly help you.
Nobody's going to make a fuss
in a case like this.'

I think I said more,
but all he did was put his face
in his hands, and mutter,
'I don't know how to put it back.'

After a moment I said,
'Forgive me, but are you *sure*
you've got it.'

I had wanted to ask the question before,
because the story did seem to be
the dream of a lunatic.
But I didn't want to hurt
poor Paxton's feelings.

lunatic – crazy
person

But he took it quite calmly,
with the calm of despair, you might say.

despair –
hopelessness

He sat up and said,
'Oh yes, there's no doubt of that.
I have it here in my room,
locked up in my bag.
You can come and look at it if you like.
I won't bring it in here.'

I wasn't likely to let the chance slip.
I went with him;
his room was only a few doors off.

There was someone
in the passage outside,
or so I thought –
afterwards I was not so sure.

Paxton was in a worse
state of shivers than before,
and went quickly into his room.
He called me after him,
turned on the light,
and shut the door carefully.

Then he unlocked his kit-bag,
and produced a bundle
in which something was wrapped.
He laid it on the bed,
and undid it.

I can now say
I have seen a real Anglo-Saxon crown.

It was of silver –
it was set with some gems,
and was of plain,
almost rough, workmanship.
In fact it was like those you see on coins.

I was very interested, of course,
and I wanted to turn it over in my hands,
but Paxton stopped me.

'Don't *you* touch it,' he said.
'I'll do that.' And with a sigh
that was dreadful to hear,
he took it up, and turned it about
so that I could see every part of it.

'Seen enough?' he said at last,
and I nodded.

He wrapped it up,
locked it in his bag,
and stood looking at me dumbly.

dumbly – here
means helplessly

'Come back to the sitting room,' I said,
'and tell me what the trouble is.'

'Oh thank you,' he said.
'Will you go first, and see if –
if the coast is clear?'

I couldn't understand why,
but I opened the door, and peered out.

fancy – here
means imagine

There was no one there,
though I did fancy a shadow
passed from one side to the other,
but I could see nothing.

'It's all right,' I whispered,
and we went back to the sitting room.

I was about to say
what a wonderful find it was,
when Paxton said,
'What is to be done?'

'Well,' I said, 'why not find out
who the owner of the land is, and . . .'

'Oh, no, no!' Paxton broke in.
'I beg your pardon,
you've been very kind,
but don't you see it's *got* to go back,
and I daren't be there at night,
and daytime's impossible.
Perhaps, though, you don't see . . .
well then, the truth is that I've never
been alone since I touched it.'

I said, 'Would it help
if you told me all about it?'

Then it all came out.

Paxton looked over his shoulder,
and called me to come nearer to him.
He began to speak in a low voice.

'It began when I was surveying the mound.
It put me off again and again.
There was always somebody – a man –
standing by one of the trees.
This was in daylight, you know.
He was never in front of me.
I always saw him out of the corner of
my eye, on the left or the right,
and he was never there
when I looked straight for him.

I lay down for quite a long time,
taking careful observations.
I made sure there was no one around,
and then when I got up
and began surveying again,
there he was.

Well, then, when I was making the tunnel,
of course it was worse.
It was like
someone scraping my back all the time.

I thought at first
it was only soil dropping on me,
but as I got nearer the – the crown,
there was no mistake!

And when I actually laid it bare,
and got my fingers round it
and pulled it out,
there came a sort of cry behind me –
oh, I can't tell you how desolate it was.
And very angry too.

desolate – unhappy
and lonely

It spoilt all my pleasure in my find.
And if I hadn't been the fool that I am,
I should have put the thing back
and left it.

But I didn't.

The rest of the time was awful.

First I had to fill up my tunnel
and cover my tracks, and all the while
he was trying to stop me.

Sometimes, you know, you see him,
and sometimes you don't – he's there,
but he has some power over your eyes.

Then I had to get back to Seaburgh,
and though it was daylight fairly soon,
that didn't make it any better.
There were always hedges,
or bushes, or fences along the road –
some sort of cover –
and I was never easy for a second.

And then when I began to meet people
going to work, they always looked
behind me very strangely.
It might have been
that they were surprised
at seeing anyone so early,
but I didn't think it was only that.
And they didn't look exactly at *me*.

Oh, you may be sure it isn't
just my imagination.

And even if I do get it put back,
he won't forgive me –
I can tell that.

And I was so happy a fortnight ago.'

He dropped into a chair,
and I believe he began to cry.

I didn't know what to say,
but I felt I must do something.
So I said if he was so set on
putting the crown back in its place,
I would help him.

That seemed the best thing to do.
If these horrible things had happened
to the poor man,
there might be something in the story
of the crown having some power
to guard the coast.

Paxton was very pleased.
He wanted to start straightaway.
He said we should not be much more
than an hour.
I looked out of the window –
there was a brilliant full moon.

And so, before I had time to think
how strange the whole thing was,
we set out.

Paxton had a large coat over his arm.
The wrapped-up crown was under it.

We went out of the hotel
into the silent town.

There was nobody about –
nobody at all.

We went past the church,
and up onto the ridge.

As we neared the mound,
I felt that there were dim presences
waiting for us.

dim presences –
things that were
there, but couldn't
be seen

Paxton felt it too.
I cannot tell you how troubled he was.
His breathing was like a hunted animal.

When we got to the mound
he flung himself at it,
and tore at it,
so that in a few minutes
he was nearly out of sight.

I stood holding his coat
and the wrapped-up crown.
I stood looking around us,
very frightened I must admit.

There was nothing to be seen –
a line of dark trees behind us,
more trees and the church tower
half a mile away,
faint barking of a dog
in a distant cottage,
calm sea dead in front,
full moon making a path across it,
and the eternal whisper
of the trees above us
and of the sea in front.

Yet in all this quiet,

acute – very sharp

I sensed an acute anger very near us.
It was just held in check,

leash – lead

like a dog on a leash
that might be let go at any moment.

Paxton pulled himself out of the hole,
and stretched his hand back to me.

'Give it to me,' he whispered,
'unwrapped.'

I pulled off the wrapping,
and he took the crown.

The moonlight fell on it
as he snatched it.
I had not myself touched
that bit of metal,
and afterwards I thought
that it was just as well.

In another moment
Paxton was out of the hole again
and busy shovelling back the soil
with hands that were already bleeding.

He wanted no help from me, though.

It was the longest part of the job
to get the place to look undisturbed.
Yet he did it very well.
At last he was satisfied,
and we turned back.

We were a couple of hundred yards
from the mound, when I looked back.
'Paxton,' I said,
'You've left your coat there. See?'

There was the long dark overcoat
lying where he had been digging.

Paxton did not stop.
He only shook his head,
and held up the coat on his arm.
'That's not my coat.'

And indeed, when I looked back again,
that dark thing was not to be seen.

Well, we got back to the road,
and came back quickly to the hotel.

The porter was there.

'Lovely night for a walk,' I said.

'You didn't meet anyone, did you sir?'

'No, indeed, not a soul,' I said.

'Only I thought I saw someone
turn onto the road behind you.'

I didn't know what to say.

Paxton just said, 'Goodnight,'
and we went off upstairs.

Back in his room,
I tried my best to cheer Paxton up.

'There's the crown safe back,' I said.
'No real harm has been done.
And don't you feel better yourself?
I don't mind saying
that on the way there
I felt we were being followed.
But, going back,
it wasn't the same at all, was it?'

But it was no good.

'*You* have nothing
to trouble yourself about,' he said,
'but I'm still not forgiven.
I've still got to pay,
I'll still have to suffer.
It's true that I don't think
he's waiting outside for me just now.
But – '

Then he stopped.

I said the best thing he could do
was sleep on it.
He would feel much better in the morning.

And it was as fine an April morning
as you could wish.
I certainly felt very different,
and Paxton also looked very different
when I saw him at breakfast.

'That's the first decent night's sleep
I've had,' he said.
'Let's go out for a walk.'

I wanted to have a bath, so I said
I would call for him in half an hour.
He agreed.

Half an hour later I knocked on his door.
He wasn't there, only his book.

Nor was he anywhere else.

I shouted for him.

The porter came out and said,
'Why, I thought you had gone out already,
and so did Mr Paxton.
He heard you calling him
from the path outside,
and ran out in a hurry.
I looked out of the window,
but I couldn't see you.
However, he ran off
down the beach that way!'

Without a word I ran that way too.
It was daylight,
there were people about,
so there was no reason, was there,
to be afraid?
Surely a man couldn't come to much harm!

I ran down to the beach.
I think I saw Paxton some distance ahead.
He seemed to be running
and waving his stick
as if he wanted to signal
to someone ahead of him.

I couldn't be sure.
A sea mist was coming up very quickly.
There was someone,
that's all I could say.

And there were tracks on the sand,
made by someone running who was in
shoes.
And there were other tracks
made by someone who was not in shoes!

Of course, it's only my word
you've got for all this,
I'd no time to make sketches or anything,
and the next tide washed everything away.
All I could do was to notice these marks
as I hurried on.

But there they were, over and over again,
and I had no doubt that what I saw
was the track of a bare foot,
and one that showed
more bones than flesh.

The mist was getting thicker and thicker.

You can guess what I was thinking – that
some *thing* had lured Paxton after it,
and that it might suddenly stop
and turn round on him,
and what sort of face might it have,
half seen at first in the mist?

And as I ran on I wondered
how Paxton could have been fooled
into mistaking that other thing for me.
I remembered him saying,
'He has some power over your eyes.'

uncanny – unnatural

It was uncanny, too,
that the sun was still bright in the sky,
but I could see nothing.

I had come to the martello tower.
Round its base was a high stone wall.
I scrambled up to the top of this wall,
to see if I could see anything
through the mist.

But I could see nothing.
I was just turning
to get down and run on,
when I heard
what I can only call a laugh.
It was, if you can understand it,
a breathless, a lungless laugh.

It came from below,
and swerved away into the mist.

That was enough.
I bent over the wall.

Paxton was there at the bottom.

You don't need to be told he was dead.
His mouth was full of sand and stones,
and his teeth and jaws
were broken to bits.
I only glanced once at his face.

Just then I heard a shout,
and a man came out of the martello tower.
He was the caretaker there.
He had seen Paxton fall and,
a moment later, seen me running up.

Had he seen anyone else?
No, he didn't think so.

He went for help,
while I stayed by the dead man
till they came with a stretcher.

inquest – inquiry
into a death

What was I to say at the inquest?

It was my duty, I felt,
to say nothing about the crown.

In the end I said just this –
that I had only met Paxton the day before,
that he had felt he was in some danger,
and that I had seen
some other tracks besides his,
when I followed him along the beach.
But of course by that time
everything had gone from the sands.

Paxton seemed to have
no family or friends.
All questions led nowhere.

And I have never been to Seaburgh,
or near it, since.